Desserts and Sweets

from around the world

Sue Ashworth

Heinemann
LIBRARY

www.heinemann.co.uk/library
Visit our website to find out more information about **Heinemann Library** books.

To order:
☎ Phone 44 (0) 1865 888066
▤ Send a fax to 44 (0) 1865 314091
💻 Visit the Heinemann Bookshop at www.heinemann.co.uk/library to browse our catalogue and order online.

First published in Great Britain by Heinemann Library, Halley Court, Jordan Hill, Oxford OX2 8EJ, part of Harcourt Education.

Heinemann is a registered trademark of Harcourt Education Ltd.

Produced for Heinemann Library by Discovery Books Ltd.
Editorial: Helena Attlee, Geoff Barker, Nancy Dickmann and Tanvi Rai
Design: Jo Hinton-Malivoire and Rob Norridge
Illustrations: Nicholas Beresford-Davies
Cartographer: Stefan Chabluk
Picture Research: Laura Durman
Production: Séverine Ribierre

Originated by Dot Gradations Ltd.
Printed in China by WKT Company Limited

ISBN 0 431 11742 X
08 07 06 05 04
10 9 8 7 6 5 4 3 2 1

British Library Cataloguing in Publication Data
Ashworth, Sue
    Desserts and Sweets from around the
        world. – (A world of recipes)
    641.8'6
A full catalogue record for this book is available from the British Library.

Acknowledgements
The Publishers would like to thank the following for permission to reproduce photographs: Bob Krist/Corbis: p.5; Terry Benson: pp. 6, **22, 23, 30, 31, 32, 33, 34, 35, 36, 37, 38, 39, 40, 41, 42, 43**; Steve Lee: pp. **10, 11, 13, 14, 15, 16, 17, 18, 19, 21, 24, 25**.

Cover photographs reproduced with permission of Terry Benson and Steve Lee.

Our thanks to Sian Davies, home economist.

Contents

Key
* * easy
* ** medium
* *** difficult

Words appearing in the text in bold, **like this**, are explained in the glossary.

Desserts around the world

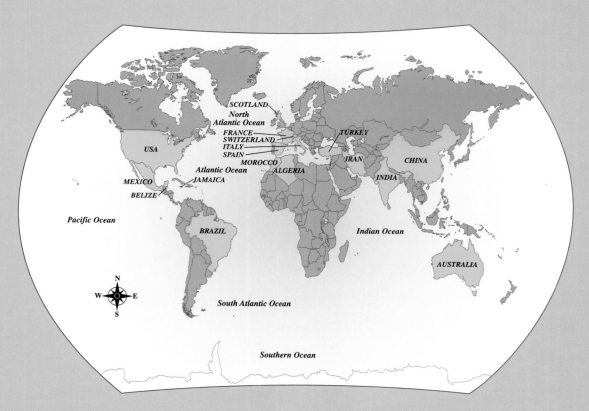

Desserts

A dessert is a delicious way to finish a meal, and every country has its own dessert recipes. Some of these recipes are very old, because people have been making desserts for a long time. In 17th-century France, for example, cooks spent days in the kitchen, creating elaborate desserts that would be displayed in towering pyramids on the king's table. There are some very special recipes in this book which come from the countries shown in yellow on the map above.

In some countries people simply use fruit as a dessert, but in other places desserts may be more complicated and time consuming to make. This difference has a lot to do with the climate and the ingredients that are readily available. If you live in a hot country where luscious tropical fruits grow, it is natural to eat them. If you live in a cold climate, where the crops are mainly cereals and orchard fruits, your dessert recipes will tend to include these ingredients.

Some cultures do not recognize the idea of a dessert as a separate course at all. In these places sweet dishes may be eaten at the same time as savoury ones.

Are desserts good for you?

Lots of the desserts in this book contain fresh fruit, which is very good for you. Fruit contains vitamins – usually vitamin C and sometimes vitamin A – which help to keep you healthy. A few of these desserts also contain cereals, such as oats and wheat in semolina, couscous and flour. These ingredients help to provide our bodies with

In the West Indies, delicious fresh fruit can be bought from open-air stalls like this one.

B vitamins and **carbohydrates**, which give the body energy. Some of these recipes also contain dairy products, such as milk, yoghurt and soft cheese, which are sources of calcium – very important for healthy teeth and bones.

Ingredients

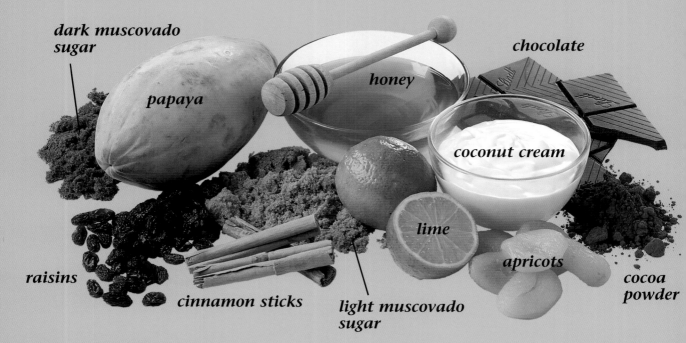

dark muscovado sugar

papaya

honey

chocolate

coconut cream

lime

apricots

cocoa powder

raisins

cinnamon sticks

light muscovado sugar

Fresh fruit

Many countries have recipes for desserts made from fruit that grows locally. In this book there is a Scottish recipe made with local raspberries, and a French recipe using cherries, one of the main fruit crops in southern France. There are other recipes using tropical and sub-tropical fruits like limes, papayas, bananas, pineapples, passion fruit and mangoes.

Dried fruit

Raisins are made from grapes that have been dried in the sun. This gives them a very concentrated flavour. Raisins or apricots can be soaked in fruit juice or water to make them even more moist and delicious. This plumps them up, and they make a lovely, simple dessert served with yoghurt and a little honey.

Cinnamon

Cinnamon is a spice used for flavouring sweet and **savoury** recipes. It is sold ground or in sticks. If you look carefully at a cinnamon stick, you will see that it is dried rolled bark. It comes from a tropical evergreen tree native to India, Sri Lanka and the Caribbean. Ground cinnamon gives a rich flavour to milk puddings, ice-cream or apple pie. You can add a cinnamon stick when **poaching** dried or fresh fruits to give a warm, spiced flavour.

Honey

The colour of honey can vary from pale, creamy white to dark brown, and it can be runny and clear or thick and cloudy. The type of flowers that the bees collect the nectar from will affect the flavour of honey. For instance, you will find that orange blossom honey has a delicate citrus flavour. Honey is the world's oldest sweetener, and it has been used in cooking for thousands of years.

Muscovado sugar

You can buy muscovado sugar in two varieties – light and dark. Light muscovado sugar has a fudgy flavour and a pale golden colour. Dark muscovado sugar has a deep, rich brown colour and a treacle-toffee taste.

Cocoa powder and chocolate

Cocoa and chocolate are used in many desserts and cakes, and are very popular in Europe and North America. Some kinds of chocolate are very sweet, and others are bitter. It is important to use the chocolate that the recipe suggests.

Coconut

Coconut milk is made by pouring boiling water over **grated** coconut flesh, then **straining** the liquid through a fine cloth. Frequently used in cooking sauces, it is available in cans. Coconut cream is thicker and is often used in desserts. Creamed coconut is a block of coconut flesh that is **melted** or grated before it is used in cooking.

Before you start

Kitchen rules

There are a few basic rules that you should always follow when you are cooking:

- Ask an adult if you can use the kitchen.
- Some cooking processes, especially those using **boiling** water or sugar, honey or oil can be very dangerous. When you see this sign, always take special care and be sure there is an adult to help you.
- Wash your hands before you start. Wipe down any surfaces with hot, soapy water.
- Wear an apron to protect your clothes, and tie back long hair.
- Be very careful when using sharp knives.
- Never leave pan handles sticking out, because you might knock the pan over.
- Always wear oven gloves to lift things in and out of the oven.
- Wash fruit and vegetables before you use them.

How long will it take?

Some of the recipes in this book are very quick and easy to make, while others are more difficult and may take much longer. The strip across the top of the right-hand page of each recipe tells you how long it will take to make each dish. It also shows you how difficult the dish is to make: every recipe in this book is either * (easy), ** (medium) or *** (quite difficult). Why not start with the easier recipes?

Quantities and measurements

You can see how much food each recipe will make at the top of each right hand page. It tells you how many people the recipe will feed. You can multiply the amounts if you want to make more but avoid changing quantities in a **baked** dish.

Ingredients in recipes can be measured in metric measurements (grams, litres and millilitres), or in imperial measurements (ounces and fluid ounces). This book uses metric measurements. If you want to convert them into imperial measurements, use the chart on page 44.

In the recipes you will see the following abbreviations:

tbsp = tablespoon	g = grams	kg = kilograms
tsp = teaspoon	ml = millilitres	cm = centimetres

Utensils

To cook these recipes you will need these utensils (as well as essentials, such as spoons, plates, bowls and serving glasses):

- baking dish
- baking sheet
- **chopping** board
- **colander**
- food processor or blender
- **grater**
- hand-held electric **beaters**
- heavy **frying** pan
- lemon squeezer
- measuring jug
- 1.5-litre ovenproof dish
- pie dish or flan dish (23cm)
- potato masher
- potato **peeler**
- **ramekin dishes**
- rolling pin
- saucepans with lids
- sharp knife
- sieve
- **slotted spoon**
- **whisk**
- **wok**

 Always take great care when using kitchen knives.

Cranachan (Scotland)

In Scotland the summers are often quite damp. These are perfect conditions for growing both raspberries and oats, the main ingredients in this delicious dessert. In this recipe, rolled oats (also called porridge oats) are **toasted** to give them a nuttier flavour.

What you need

50g rolled oats
   (porridge oats)
250g fresh raspberries
300ml double cream
4 tbsp runny honey
a few mint leaves

What you do

1 Turn the grill on to a medium heat.

2 **Sprinkle** the rolled oats on to a **baking** sheet and spread them out evenly.

(!) 3 Carefully toast the oats under the grill until they are light brown. This will take 2–3 minutes. Keep an eye on them to make sure that they don't burn. With an adult's help, remove the baking sheet from under the grill and allow the oats to **cool**.

4 Put half the raspberries into a bowl. Use a fork or potato masher to squash them down slightly, until they have a soft, mushy texture.

5 Save 8 whole raspberries for decoration. Put the rest of the whole raspberries into 4 serving glasses.

6 Pour the cream into a large mixing bowl. Use a **whisk** to **whip** the cream until it thickens. Tip the crushed raspberries and toasted oats into the whipped cream. Add the honey. Stir gently together.

7 Spoon the cream mixture into the serving glasses. Decorate each of them with 2 raspberries and some mint leaves. Serve the desserts immediately, or **cover** and put in the fridge until you are ready to eat them.

Key lime pie (USA)

In the southern states of the USA, especially Florida, citrus fruits are grown to enjoy locally, to send to other parts of the country, and to **export** to other countries. This favourite dessert originates from the Florida Keys, where limes are grown.

What you need

75g butter
150g digestive biscuits
3 limes
3 medium eggs
1 x 405g can condensed milk
50g caster sugar

What you do

1 **Melt** the butter in a large saucepan over a low heat.

2 Put the biscuits into a large polythene bag. Use a rolling pin to crush the biscuits into crumbs. Tip these into the melted butter and use a wooden spoon to stir them well.

3 Tip the biscuit crumbs into a 23cm pie or flan dish. Press them over the base and up the sides of the dish, taking care as the butter may still be hot. Chill in the fridge for about 15 minutes.

4 **Preheat** the oven to 180°C/350°F/gas mark 4. Finely **grate** the **peel** and squeeze the juice from the limes.

5 Separate the eggs, putting the yolks in a medium-sized bowl and the whites in a large bowl. Pour the condensed milk into the egg yolks and **beat** together. Stir in the grated lime peel and juice.

6 Pour the egg yolk mixture over the chilled biscuit crumb base. Place in the oven and **bake** for 15–20 minutes, until it has set.

7 **Whip** the egg whites until they hold their shape – this takes about 3–4 minutes. Add the sugar bit by bit, **whisking** well every time you add it. The whites will form stiff, glossy peaks.

8 Pile this meringue topping on to the lime pie. Return it to the oven and bake for about 8–10 minutes, until the surface is golden brown. **Cool**, and then serve in slices.

SEPARATING EGGS

Crack each egg into a clean bowl. Separate by using a clean spoon to gently lift out the yolk.

Pistachio ice-cream (Iran)

Pistachio nuts were originally grown in the Middle East, so they are a popular ingredient in both sweet and **savoury** dishes in Iran, Lebanon, Syria and Afghanistan. They are attractive nuts, with beautiful purple skins and pale green flesh in a tough outer shell.

What you need

200g shelled pistachio nuts (unsalted)
600ml ready-made custard (or vanilla pudding)
50g caster sugar
1 tsp vanilla extract
1 tsp almond essence
300ml double cream
3–4 drops green food colouring (optional)

What you do

1 Put the pistachio nuts into a blender or food processor. Blend them for about 15–20 seconds until they are very finely **chopped**. Tip them into a large bowl.

2 Pour the custard or vanilla pudding into the bowl with the nuts. Stir in the sugar, vanilla **extract** and almond **essence**.

3 Pour the double cream into a large mixing bowl. Use a **whisk** to **whip** the cream until it thickens. Add 3–4 drops of food colouring if you wish, stirring it in to give a pale green colour, but be careful not to add too much.

4 Stir the vanilla mixture, then tip it into the bowl of whipped cream. Use a large metal spoon to **fold** the cream and custard together until they are evenly mixed.

5 Tip the mixture into a rigid freezer container. Freeze for about 1 hour until the mixture has started to freeze around the edges of the container.

6 Using a whisk or a fork, stir the mixture well to break down the ice crystals. Return to the freezer and freeze until solid – about 2 more hours.

7 To serve, take the ice-cream from the freezer about 15 minutes before you want to eat it, so that it is soft enough to scoop easily.

Tiramisù (Italy)

Tiramisù is an Italian dessert that originally came from Venice. Its name translates as 'pick-me-up' and it is made with a fresh, soft Italian cream cheese called mascarpone. It is a popular dessert in Italian restaurants all over the world.

What you need

4 tsp coffee granules
  or powder
300g mascarpone cheese
150ml single cream
25g caster sugar
1 tsp vanilla extract
12 sponge fingers
1 tsp cocoa powder

What you do

1 Mix the coffee granules or powder into 150ml of very hot water. Stir until dissolved, then pour into a shallow bowl.

2 In another bowl, use a wooden spoon to stir the mascarpone cheese and single cream together. Add the sugar and vanilla **extract** and stir until thoroughly mixed in.

3 Before you start to assemble the desserts, line up 4 small–medium serving glasses, or use **ramekin dishes**. You can even use teacups instead.

4 Cut the sponge fingers in half and divide them into 2 equal piles. Dip 1 pile of sponge fingers, 1 at a time, briefly into the coffee mixture, then place them in the base of the glasses or ramekin dishes. You need to put 3 pieces into each dish.

5 Spoon half of the mascarpone mixture into the serving glasses. Now dip the rest of the sponge fingers into the coffee and put them in the glasses. Again, you will need to put 3 pieces in each one. Spoon in the rest of the mixture and level the surface so that it is smooth.

6 **Sprinkle** each dessert with a little cocoa powder. **Cover** them with cling-film and chill them in the fridge until you are ready to serve them.

7 Remove the desserts from the fridge about 10 minutes before you want to eat them, so that they are not too cold.

Cherry clafoutis (France)

This cherry **batter** pudding comes from the Limousin region of central France. Traditionally, the first cherries of the season would be used to create this dessert. It comes out of the oven puffed up and golden brown.

What you need

15g butter
500g fresh cherries
100g plain flour
pinch of salt
2 eggs
1 tsp vanilla extract
250ml milk
40g caster sugar
10g icing sugar
200ml single cream

What you do

1 **Preheat** the oven to 190°C/375°F/gas mark 5.

2 Grease a 1.5-litre shallow, ovenproof dish with the butter. The dish should measure approximately 20 x 30cm.

3 Add the cherries to the buttered **baking** dish. You could remove their stones first, if you like, although the cherries keep their shape better if you leave them in.

4 Put the flour, salt, eggs, vanilla **extract** and milk into a bowl and **beat** together with a **whisk** to make a smooth batter. Add the caster sugar and stir it in. Let the mixture stand for a few minutes so that the sugar dissolves.

5 Stir the batter, then pour it over the cherries. Carefully transfer the dish to the oven and bake for 30–35 minutes, until the batter has puffed up and turned golden brown. With an adult's help, carefully remove the dish from the oven.

6 Put the icing sugar into a sieve and **sift** it over the pudding. Serve the pudding, accompanied by a jug of single cream. If you haven't removed the stones from the cherries, be sure to warn your guests.

OTHER FRUIT

Clafoutis is traditionally made with cherries, but you can experiment with other fruits as well. Plums, peaches and apricots are a good substitute for cherries, but you will need to cut them in half and remove their stones.

Mango shrikhand (India)

Mango desserts are extremely popular in India, where the ripe, juicy fruits are very refreshing in the hot summer months. Indian desserts are often made with dairy foods, like this one.

What you need

1kg set natural yoghurt
3 tbsp milk
pinch of saffron strands
2 large ripe mangoes
50g caster sugar
½ tsp ground cardamom
½ tsp ground nutmeg
to decorate, a few mint
  leaves

What you do

1 Dampen a large piece of fine cotton muslin or a new, disposable dish-cloth with water and then wring it out well. Place it in a large sieve or **colander**, and then position this over a large bowl.

2 Stir the yoghurt, then tip it into the cloth. Knot the opposite corners of the cloth together. Chill in the fridge for about 6 hours, or overnight if you prefer. The yoghurt will thicken and a clear liquid will drip through the cloth into the bowl.

3 Next day, heat the milk until it almost **boils**. Remove from the heat. Add the **saffron strands** and allow to **infuse** for 20–30 minutes to give a bright yellow liquid.

4 Empty the yoghurt from the cloth into a large bowl. Throw away the thin liquid that has dripped through the cloth.

5 Now prepare the mangoes. Ask an adult to help you cut through the flesh on either side of the stone with a sharp knife. This is the only way that the stone can be removed properly.

(!) **6 Peel** the mangoes with a potato peeler, or scoop the flesh from the skin with a spoon. **Purée** their flesh in a food processor or blender for about 15 seconds.

7 Add the puréed mangoes to the yoghurt, and stir in the sugar, cardamom and nutmeg. Add the milk, pouring it through a small sieve to remove the saffron. Stir well, then spoon the mixture into 6 serving dishes. Decorate each dessert with the mint leaves.

Cool orange granita (Algeria)

In the blistering heat of an Algerian summer, people enjoy cooling desserts to refresh and revive them. This granita, which is like a rough-textured sorbet, is typical of North African desserts.

What you need

1 litre unsweetened orange juice

2 tbsp lemon juice

250g unrefined caster sugar

¼ tsp ground cinnamon

2 tbsp orange flower water or rosewater (optional)

to decorate, thin strips of orange peel and some mint leaves

What you do

1 In a large jug, mix together the orange juice, lemon juice and caster sugar. Add the cinnamon, orange flower water, or rosewater if you are using them.

2 Let the mixture stand for a few minutes to make sure that the sugar has completely dissolved. Stir once more.

3 Pour the orange juice mixture into a shallow, plastic freezer box. Transfer to the freezer and freeze for about an hour.

4 Remove from the freezer. By now, ice crystals will have started to form around the edge of the container. Break these up with a fork and stir well. Return to the freezer.

5 Repeat this procedure of breaking up the ice crystals every 45 minutes or so, to give a light crunchy texture. Keep in the freezer until you want to serve it.

6 To serve the granita, scoop the mixture into serving glasses. Decorate with thin strips of orange **peel** and a few mint leaves.

23

Grilled papaya with lime (Mexico)

A papaya is an exotic fruit grown in tropical countries. The papaya has other names too, so you may see it called a *papaw*, or a melon *zapote*.

What you need

1 large papaya
1 lime
3 tbsp dark muscovado sugar
50g cream cheese
5 tbsp strawberry yoghurt

What you do

1 **Slice** the papaya in half, lengthways. Use a teaspoon to scoop out all the black seeds and throw these away.

2 **Peel** the papaya halves using a potato peeler, then use a sharp knife to cut each papaya half into about 6 or 7 slices. Arrange the papaya slices on a **baking** sheet. Throw away the peel.

3 Cut the lime in half and squeeze the juice into a small bowl. Add 2 tbsp of sugar. Stir the sugar in and then leave to dissolve into a **syrup**.

4 Mix the cream cheese with the strawberry yoghurt.

5 **Preheat** the grill. **Sprinkle** the papaya slices with the remaining sugar. Put the baking sheet under the grill and cook the papaya slices for about 3 minutes, so that the sugar begins to bubble.

6 With an adult's help, remove the baking sheet from the grill and **cool** for 2 minutes.

7 Carefully lift the papaya slices on to 2 serving plates. Spoon the lime syrup over them, then serve them with the strawberry yoghurt mixture.

Ground almond pudding (Turkey)

Dried fruits and nuts often feature in Turkish cookery, and milk puddings made with semolina or ground rice are very popular. This delicious recipe is a combination of milk, semolina, dried fruits and flaked almonds that have been lightly **toasted**.

What you need

4 ready-to-eat dried
    apricots
4 tsp toasted flaked
    almonds
50g semolina
600ml milk
15g butter
50g ground almonds
25g sultanas
1 tsp vanilla extract
40g caster sugar

What you do

1 **Slice** the apricots into about 8 thin pieces – you can do this with scissors, if you like. Mix them with the toasted flaked almonds. Set to one side.

2 Put the semolina into a medium-sized, non-stick saucepan and pour in the milk. Heat gently, stirring all the time with a **whisk** or a wooden spoon. The mixture will thicken as it comes up to the **boil**.

3 Reduce the heat and cook gently for 2 minutes, stirring all the time.

4 Take the saucepan off the heat and stir in the butter, ground almonds, sultanas, vanilla **extract** and sugar. Pour the mixture into 4 serving dishes.

5 **Sprinkle** the top of each pudding with the almonds and apricots, then serve at once.

TOASTING ALMONDS

Toasting nuts brings out their flavour. To toast nuts yourself, spread them on a **baking** sheet and put them under a medium grill for about 2 minutes.

27

Passion fruit mousse (Brazil)

The passion fruit has lots of different names – in many countries it is called a *grenadilla* and in Brazil it is called a *maracuja*. The fruit grows on flowering vines, native to the rainforests of Brazil.

What you need

6 ripe passion fruit
300g condensed milk
300ml double cream
1 tbsp lemon juice

What you do

1 Put 2 passion fruit to one side. Cut the remaining fruits in half, then scoop the seeds and **pulp** into a bowl.

2 Measure the condensed milk into a mixing bowl.

3 Tip the passion fruit seeds and pulp into a sieve. Using a large spoon, push the pulp through the sieve into the bowl with the condensed milk, leaving the black seeds in the sieve to be thrown away.

4 Pour the double cream into another mixing bowl. Use a **whisk** to **whip** the cream until it thickens.

5 Spoon the cream into the bowl with the condensed milk. **Fold** everything together gently so that it is evenly mixed. Add the lemon juice and stir this through.

28

6 Spoon the mixture into 4 serving glasses. **Cover** and chill in the fridge until you want to eat them.

7 Just before serving the desserts, cut the 2 remaining passion fruits in half. Using a teaspoon, scoop the seeds and pulp on to the desserts, allowing half for each portion.

CHOOSING RIPE FRUIT

Passion fruit are at their best when the skin is wrinkled – this is a sign that they are ripe and fragrant. The crunchy black seeds, surrounded by citrus pulp, are edible.

Tropical fruit with cinnamon cream (Jamaica)

All the fruits in this delicious dessert are grown in the tropical climate of the Caribbean. Here the hot sunshine is followed by heavy rainfall, giving lush vegetation and abundant crops.

What you need

1 ripe papaya
1 mango
2 bananas
227g can pineapple
   slices in natural juice
25g butter
50g light muscovado
   sugar
150ml double cream
100ml coconut cream
   or coconut milk
pinch of cinnamon

What you do

1 **Slice** the papaya in half, lengthways. Use a teaspoon to scoop out all the black seeds and throw them away. **Peel** the papaya halves and then, with an adult's help, use a sharp knife to cut each papaya half into 6 slices.

2 Cut through the flesh on either side of the mango stone with a sharp knife. Peel the fruit with a potato peeler, and then cut the flesh into slices.

3 Peel and slice the bananas. Drain the pineapple, reserving the juice, and slice each ring in half.

4 **Melt** the butter in a large **frying** pan. Turn down the heat and add the sugar. Stir the sugar and butter together, add the pineapple juice and cook gently until the sugar has dissolved.

5 Add the papaya, mango, bananas and pineapples to the frying pan and stir gently. Cook over a low heat for 3–4 minutes, stirring occasionally.

6 Pour the double cream into a mixing bowl. Use a **whisk** to **whip** it until it thickens. **Fold** in the coconut cream or coconut milk and cinnamon.

7 Share out the fruit and **syrupy** juices between 4 serving plates or bowls and serve with the cinnamon cream.

WHIPPING CREAM

Take care when you whip cream. You must stop as soon as it becomes thick. If you go on for too long it might separate, and then you will not be able to whip it up again.

Peach Melba (Australia)

This recipe was originally created by a famous French chef called Escoffier, who used to be the chef at the Savoy Hotel in London. He created the dessert in 1893 as a tribute to Dame Nellie Melba, a famous Australian opera singer.

What you need

200g caster sugar
4 peaches
200g fresh or frozen
(thawed) raspberries
4 scoops vanilla ice-
cream

What you do

(!) 1 Put the sugar and 500ml water into a large pan. Heat gently to dissolve the sugar.

2 **Slice** the peaches in half. The easiest way to do this is to cut around the whole peach, through the end where the stalk was, then twist the 2 halves in opposite directions to separate them. Remove the stones.

3 Put the peach halves into the saucepan and **simmer** them for about 5 minutes until they are **tender**. Remove the pan from the heat.

(!) 4 Put the raspberries into a food processor or blender. Add 4 tbsp of **syrup** from the peaches. Blend for about 15 seconds until smooth.

5 **Strain** the raspberry **purée** through a sieve into a jug or bowl, so that it is smooth.

6 Lift the peaches into 4 serving dishes with a **slotted spoon**. You can **peel** them if you're not keen on the skins. Add a little syrup from the peaches to each dish. Top each portion with a scoop of vanilla ice-cream, then pour some raspberry sauce over each of them. Serve at once.

Pineapple and sesame fritters (China)

In China, fruit fritters are a popular dessert. The best way to cook them is in a **wok**, a deep, curved cooking pot, but you can use a deep-sided **frying** pan instead.

What you need

425g can pineapple
   rings in natural juice
200g plain flour
pinch of salt
1 large egg
1 tbsp groundnut oil
150ml vegetable oil,
   for frying
4 tbsp clear honey
1½ heaped tsp sesame
   seeds

What you do

1 Drain the can of pineapples really well. You don't need the juice for the recipe, so you can drink it if you like. Put the pineapple rings on to double-thickness sheets of kitchen paper to drain.

2 **Sprinkle** 3 tbsp flour on to a plate. Dip the pineapple rings into the flour to coat them lightly.

3 To make the **batter**, put 100g flour, salt, egg and 120ml water into a mixing bowl. **Beat** with a **whisk** to make a smooth batter, then stir in the groundnut oil.

(!) 4 Pour the vegetable oil into a wok or frying pan and carefully heat it.

(!) 5 Dip a pineapple ring into the batter. Use a **slotted spoon** to lift it out, and let some of the batter drain off. Put it into the frying pan. Be careful, as the oil may spatter. Do the same with another 1 or 2 rings.

(!) 6 When the pineapple rings have cooked for about a minute, turn them over. When they are light golden brown, lift them out with the slotted spoon. Place them on sheets of kitchen paper to drain. Repeat with the remaining rings.

7 Serve the fritters drizzled with the honey and sprinkled with sesame seeds.

Sweet potato pudding (Belize)

Sweet potatoes were originally grown in Belize, Mexico and Peru, but now they grow in many other hot places. The sweet potato was one of the first vegetables to be brought across the Atlantic from the New World by Christopher Columbus.

What you need

25g butter
700g sweet potatoes
400ml coconut milk
250g caster sugar
3 medium eggs
170g can evaporated milk
2 tsp vanilla extract
50g raisins
½ tsp ground ginger
single cream, to serve

What you do

1 **Preheat** the oven to 180°C/350°F/gas mark 4. Grease a 1.5-litre **baking** dish with a teaspoon of the butter.

2 **Peel** the sweet potatoes, then **grate** them and put them into a large mixing bowl with the coconut milk and sugar. Stir well.

(!) 3 **Melt** the remaining butter in a small saucepan, then add it to the sweet potato mixture.

4 **Beat** the eggs in a bowl and add these to the mixture. Add the evaporated milk, vanilla **extract**, raisins and ground ginger. Stir well.

5 Pour the potato mixture into the prepared baking dish. Ask an adult to help you put it on the middle shelf of the oven. Bake for 45 minutes.

6 Spoon into serving dishes and serve on its own, or with some thick cream if you prefer.

SWEET AND SAVOURY

Sweet potatoes have sweet flesh, which is how they got their name. However, they are usually used in **savoury** dishes, and so this recipe is quite unusual.

Fruity couscous (Morocco)

Couscous is one of Morocco's **staple** foods. It is usually served with spicy stews called *tagines*, but in this sweet dish it is served with a warm fruit salad, made with North African fruit.

What you need

200g couscous
15g butter
150g ready-to-eat dried
  apricots
50g sultanas or raisins
50g dates
3 oranges
100g light muscovado
  sugar
½ tsp ground nutmeg
1½ tsp vanilla extract

What you do

1 Put the couscous into a large saucepan and **cover** it with 350ml of just-**boiled** water. Add the butter and stir it in. Cook over a low heat for 2 minutes. Remove from the heat, cover with the lid and leave to swell for about 15 minutes.

2 Put the apricots and sultanas or raisins into a saucepan. **Slice** the dates in half. Remove the stones and throw them away. Add the dates to the pan.

3 Finely **grate** the **peel** from 1 orange, and then squeeze the juice from it. Reserve the grated peel and add the juice to the fruit.

4 Add 150ml of cold water and 50g of the sugar to the fruit. **Simmer** over a low heat for 10 minutes.

5 Stir the couscous with a fork to fluff up the grains. Add the peel, ground nutmeg, vanilla **extract** and the rest of the sugar. Stir to mix everything together.

6 Peel the remaining oranges, removing as much of the **pith** as possible. Cut them into slices across the segments. Add these slices to the fruit salad.

7 Serve the couscous and spoon the fruit salad on top.

Flan (Spain)

These delicious egg custards appear on every menu in Spanish restaurants – and they are cooked in Spanish homes, too. The method in this recipe may be a little different to the traditional one, but is just as delicious.

What you need

600ml milk
3 large eggs
3 egg yolks
1 tsp vanilla extract
50g caster sugar
8 tsp light
    muscovado sugar

What you do

1 **Preheat** the oven to 180°C/350°F/gas mark 4.

2 Heat the milk very gently until it is lukewarm.

3 In a large jug, **beat** together the eggs, egg yolks, vanilla **extract** and caster sugar. Carefully pour in the milk, stirring all the time. Keep stirring the mixture for a few minutes to dissolve the sugar.

4 Using a fine sieve, **strain** the liquid into 4 **ramekin dishes** or small **baking** dishes.

5 Place the dishes in a large rectangular baking dish or roasting pan. Pour warm water around the dishes, to reach half way up their sides. Carefully transfer this to the middle shelf of the oven.

6 Bake the desserts until they are set. They will take 25–30 minutes. If they still look wobbly in the middle, cook for a few minutes longer.

7 About 10 minutes before serving, **sprinkle** the top of each dessert with 2 tsp of muscovado sugar. This will **melt** to form a delicious, caramel-flavoured sauce.

BAKING IN WATER

Baking the desserts in water means that they cook in a steady, gentle heat that will help the custards to stay smooth and creamy. In Spain, small earthenware dishes are often used.

Chocolate mousse (Switzerland)

Some of the best chocolate in the world is made in Switzerland. The rich milk produced by cows grazing on the country's lush pastures helps to give Swiss chocolate its wonderful flavour.

What you need

100g dark Swiss
    chocolate
1 tbsp cocoa powder
4 tbsp cornflour
300ml milk
50g granulated sugar
to decorate, a few
    mint leaves

What you do

1 Break the chocolate into squares and put it into a non-stick saucepan.

2 In a mixing bowl, mix together the cocoa powder and cornflour. Add the milk a little at a time, stirring the mixture with a wooden spoon to blend the ingredients together.

(!) 3 Add the milk mixture to the chocolate. Heat gently, stirring all the time with a small **whisk** or wooden spoon. As the mixture heats, the chocolate will **melt** and blend into the other ingredients. Keep the pan on a low heat until the mixture becomes very thick. Do not stop stirring!

4 Add the sugar to the chocolate mixture.

5 Spoon the mousse into 4 very small glasses or tiny teacups. Scatter mint leaves over them to decorate. Let them **cool**, then **cover** and chill in the fridge until you are ready to serve them.

QUALITY CHOCOLATE

The best chocolate for cooking contains at least 70 per cent cocoa solids, so check the wrapper before you buy it.

Further information

Here are some books and websites that will help you to find out more about foods used in desserts from around the world.

Books

The Latin American Kitchen, Elisabeth Luard (Kyle Cathie Limited, 2002).
Seductive Flavours of the Levant, Nada Saleh (Robson, 2002).

Websites

http://www.ability.org.uk/kids_recipes.html
http://kid.allrecipes.com

Conversion chart

Ingredients for recipes can be measured in two different ways. Metric measurements use grams and millilitres. Imperial measurements use ounces and fluid ounces. This book uses metric measurements. The chart here shows you how to convert measurements from metric to imperial.

SOLIDS		LIQUIDS	
METRIC	IMPERIAL	METRIC	IMPERIAL
10g	1/4 oz	30ml	1 fl oz
15g	1/2 oz	50ml	2 fl oz
25g	1 oz	75ml	2 1/2 fl oz
50g	1 3/4 oz	100ml	3 1/2 fl oz
75g	2 3/4 oz	125ml	4 fl oz
100g	3 1/2 oz	150ml	5 fl oz
150g	5 oz	300ml	10 fl oz
250g	9 oz	600ml	20 fl oz
450g	1 lb	900ml	30 fl oz

Healthy eating

This diagram shows you what foods you should eat to stay healthy. Most of your food should come from the bottom of the pyramid. Eat some of the foods from the middle every day. Only eat a little of the foods from the top.

Healthy eating should be a balance of all kinds of different foods, so it's fine to enjoy a dessert every so often, but remember that it's not a good idea to eat too much sugar, as sugar is bad for your teeth, and it can also make you put on too much weight.

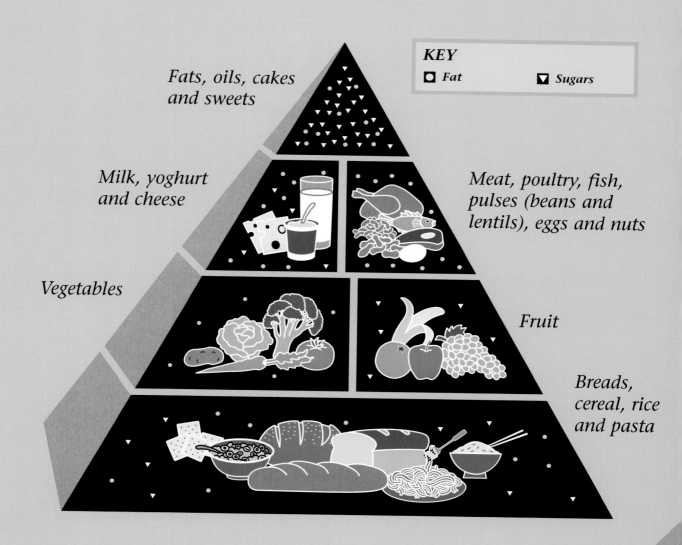

Fats, oils, cakes and sweets

KEY
☐ *Fat*　　▽ *Sugars*

Milk, yoghurt and cheese

Meat, poultry, fish, pulses (beans and lentils), eggs and nuts

Vegetables

Fruit

Breads, cereal, rice and pasta

Glossary

bake cook something, such as cakes or pies, in the oven

batter mixture of flour, eggs and liquid or fat, used to make cakes or pancakes

beat mix something together strongly, using a fork, spoon or whisk

boil cook a liquid on the hob (or the flat top part of the cooker). Boiling liquid bubbles and begins to steam.

carbohydrate starchy sugar found in bread, potatoes, etc.

chop cut something into pieces, using a knife or blender

colander bowl-shaped container with holes in it, used for straining vegetables and draining

cool allow hot food to become cold. You should always allow food to cool before putting it in the fridge.

cover put a lid on a pan, or foil or cling-film over a dish

essence very strong flavouring. You need only a small drop of essence, while you may need a teaspoonful of extract.

export sell a product, such as fruit, to another country

extract a flavouring, such as vanilla or almond extract

fold gently mix a light, airy mixture into a heavier one

fry cook something in oil in a pan

grate cut into small pieces, using a grater

infuse soak something so that its flavour and/or colour is released

melt change from solid to liquid when heated

peel remove the skin of a fruit or vegetable; or the skin itself (also known as rind or zest)

pith white part of the skin of citrus fruits

poach cook by boiling gently in a little liquid

preheat turn the oven or grill on in advance, so that it is hot when you are ready to heat the food

pulp the soft, moist part of the fruit

purée mash, sieve, liquidize or blend food until it is smooth; or the blended food itself

ramekin dish small straight-sided dish, suitable for baking, used for making individual portions

saffron strand dried stigma (part of the flower that receives pollen during pollination) of a particular type of crocus, used to give a yellow colour and delicate flavour to desserts, cakes and savoury dishes

savoury salty rather than sweet flavour

sift shake an ingredient, such as flour, through a sieve

simmer boil gently

slice cut something into thin, flat pieces

slotted spoon large spoon with holes in it that allows you to drain the food as you lift it

sprinkle scatter small pieces or drops on to something

staple one of the most important foods in a person's diet is called a staple food, such as bread, rice or potatoes

strain pour a liquid through a sieve. If it has bits of fruit or seeds in it, straining the liquid can get rid of them.

syrup a thick, sweet liquid made from sugar and water

tender soft, but not squashy

toast heat under a grill or in a toaster

whip beat an ingredient, such as cream, to make it light and airy

whisk beating ingredients to make them light and airy, or utensil used for doing this

wok a deep, curved cooking pot, mainly used for stir-frying, especially in Chinese and Southeast Asian cookery

Index

Titles in the *A World of Recipes* series include:

A World of Recipes

Christmas Foods

Jenny Vaughan and Penny Beauchamp

Hardback   0 431 11739 X

A World of Recipes

Festival Foods

Jenny Vaughan and Penny Beauchamp

Hardback   0 431 11740 3

A World of Recipes

Snacks
from around the world

Sue Ashworth

Hardback   0 431 11741 1

A World of Recipes

Desserts and Sweets
from around the world

Sue Ashworth

Hardback   0 431 11742 X

Find out about the other titles in this series on our website www.heinemann.co.uk/library